APOCKETFUL
OFAPARTMENTS

APOCKETFUL
OFAPARTMENTS

Edited by Janelle McCulloch

images
Publishing

Published in Australia in 2007 by
The Images Publishing Group Pty Ltd
ABN 89 059 734 431
6 Bastow Place, Mulgrave, Victoria, 3170, Australia
Telephone +61 9561 5544 Facsimile +61 9561 4860
Email: books@images.com.au
Website: www.imagespublishing.com

National Library of Australia
Cataloguing-in-Publication entry:

A pocketful of apartments

Includes index
ISBN 978 186470 256 9

1. Apartments - Pictorial works. 2. Interior architecture. 3. Interior decoration.
I. McCulloch, Janelle. II. The Images Publishing Group.

643.27

Coordinating Editor: Janelle McCulloch

Designed by The Graphic Image Studio Pty Ltd, Mulgrave, Australia
Website: www.tgis.com.au

Printed by Everbest Printing Co. Ltd., in Hong Kong/China

IMAGES has included on its website a page for special notices in relation to this and our other publications.
Please visit this site: www.imagespublishing.com

CONTENTS

CONTENTS

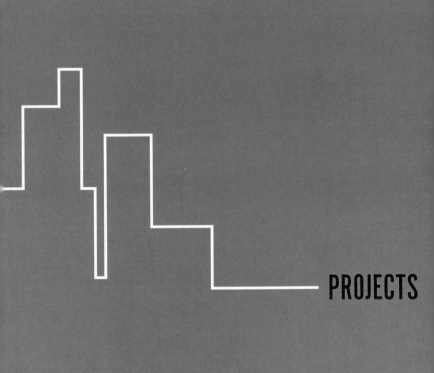

PROJECTS

13TH STREET RESIDENCE

Marble Fairbanks Architects

The owner of this residence, previously an art director, is a collector of American folk art. The program was to incorporate his art collection into the design of this one-bedroom, 1800-square-foot, second-floor loft. A range of materials was used to set up episodic scenes to both frame the art and choreograph movement through the space. The ceiling height allowed the architects to insert a library mezzanine with suspended steel shelves and a minimal steel walkway that bridges the space, dividing more public living from the private bedroom/dressing/bathroom suite.

Material transparency, reflectivity, and a variety of textured opacities expand and reconfigure spatial relationships. The material palette includes blackened hot-rolled steel plates, etched glass, dyed fiber board, poured-in-place concrete, ebonized cherry and plaster for wall surfaces, and slate, limestone and oak for floor surfaces.

A PLACE IN THE SUN

André Piva Arquitetura

For his own apartment, architect André Piva used a restrained design strategy to create an ethereal 'vacation' environment, and the neutral palette provided a perfect backdrop to the fantastic view of Rio.

For this architect the most important design factor, excluding the external environment, was the concept of a loft. The three-level, 500-square-meter apartment is located in the heart of Rio, in the Rodrigo de Freitas lagoon. The first floor accommodates the master bedroom and the guest room. The second floor is the living area, with the living, dining, and the American kitchen in one area. The spectacular terrace, complete with swimming pool and views of Corcovado and the statue of Christ, is also on the second floor. The service area, family room, and library, are on the third-floor mezzanine.

The stripped-back, clean design with its white walls and limestone floors, deliberately eliminated extraneous features. White aluminum and brushed steel contribute to the minimalist color palette of white, off-white, and black.

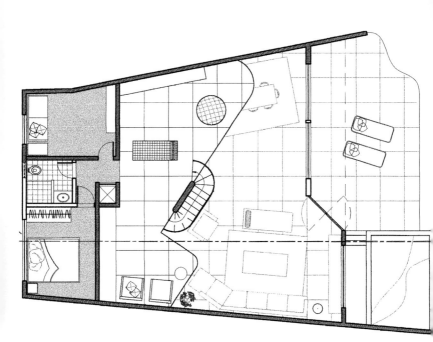

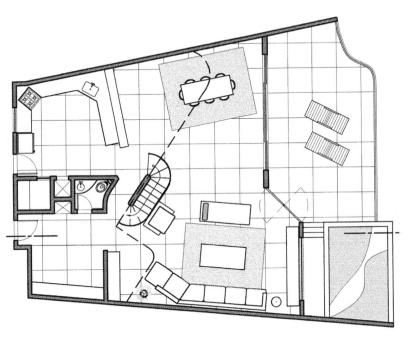

19

APARTMENT 15

Jackson Clements Burrows Architects

Apartment 15 is located on the top floor of the AKM building, one of a small group of significant brick warehouses that formerly housed a range of textile-related industries.

The 210-square-meter apartment is divided into two main volumes spread over four levels. A fifth level accommodates a 40-square-meter roof deck, boasting uninterrupted views of the city skyline and surrounding parklands.

The first two levels sit within the existing glazed sawtooth roof and benefit from extensive natural lighting. The lower (entry) level accommodates an open-plan living area and linear strip kitchen. The next level houses a study/bedroom while a generous bathroom contains an inset bath set against a glazed truss with stainless steel benches responding to the industrial heritage of the original building.

Continuing upstairs, one leaves the first volume and passes out of the main building into the second volume housed on the bridge structure over the laneway. This space within the original bridge structure accommodates the master bedroom and an additional bedroom fronting the south side. Polished black butt stairs lead to the retreat lounge on the fourth level. The entire western wall is glazed with sliding door panels that retract to a cantilevered position beyond the walls overhanging the laneway below. Solar gain from this west-facing retractable glazed wall was a concern and a series of external, computer-controlled retractable aluminium louvers were installed to address this issue. Further sensors assess wind loads and retract the aluminium louvers when wind speeds are excessive, protecting the system from damage.

A further stair extends upward. Rising from a series of layered timber platforms, the stair arrives at a precarious landing hovering in front of a blue glazed, 5-meter corner window. The unnerving view down into the laneway some 20 meters below is only relieved by the expansive roof deck, which unfolds to uninterrupted views in all directions.

APARTMENT FOR AN AUTHOR

Centerbrook Architects and Planners

This project involved the renovation of a foyer, dining room, and library/writing studio in a New York duplex apartment. The client, a noted author, wanted the interior to be elegant, yet comfortable and efficient for her daily chore of putting words to paper. She also desired a work of invention, superior craftsmanship, and lasting value.

Sitting below the upper penthouse floor, which is glassy and light, the renovation offers a counterpoint—a vaulted retreat—a place to dine on cold winter nights and to work year-round, hidden away from the world.

Working within a shell of uninspired gypsum board box spaces, new ceilings, cabinets, and columns were created from teak and rendered in an invented classic style. Teak is easy to work with, allowing high relief. While it appears warm, the coloration has a slight green cast that accentuates its modeling and the craft of the cabinetmaker. A deep terracotta red was chosen as the color behind the walls to contrast to the teak while lighting was hidden in the column capitals to give the ceilings a soft glow at night. Desks and bookshelves, meanwhile, were designed with great care, offering 'a place for everything and everything in its place.' Some drawers are shallow with felt liners and folding metal rods to hold down loose stacks of typed pages. These allow the writer to have readily available book chapters in semi-disarray and yet be able to 'close up shop' at a moment's notice.

In the middle of the three spaces is a staircase with Art Nouveau-like wrought iron railings leading up to the penthouse. A few shallow steps at the window end of the library lead up to a raised platform with a view of Central Park beyond.

The final result of all this effort is an apartment with a strong sense of itself. Designed to withstand the whims of an inveterate collector, it still has enough character to meld eclectic origins and become a remarkable place of its own.

BRITTON STREET PENTHOUSE

Form Design Architecture

The elliptical upper floor of this luxurious 2900-square-foot duplex penthouse in London is a prominent local landmark, commanding spectacular panoramic city views to St Paul's Cathedral.

Carved out of the sixth- and seventh-floor shell spaces originally earmarked for two apartments by the developer, the spatial arrangement has been conceived around a route that draws the visitor through the apartment from the point of entry on the lower floor to the final revelation of the 360-degree view from the upper floor living space and covered alfresco dining area on the landscaped terrace.

A linear entry gallery terminates in an atrium area at the heart of the plan, which links the two floors of open-plan living space. A double-height wall plate rises through this volume, tracing the curved perimeter of the upper floor ellipse, and linking the disparate geometries of the two levels. The wall also provides a degree of enclosure, and acts as a backdrop for the central focus of the apartment: an elegant cantilevered oak and glass stair. Ascending the stair, the curve of the enclosing wall gently turns the visitor through 180 degrees to finally reveal the spectacular city view, focused on St Paul's to the south from the upper level living area and terrace.

On the lower floor, a bedroom wing is linked to the open-plan living/entertaining areas via a transitional space: a cozy, book-lined study located behind a sliding wall. When required, this can be closed to create a third bedroom—complete with bathroom discreetly concealed behind built-in joinery. The master suite and a further guest suite are also essentially open plan, but are fully divisible (when guests are staying) with a system of concealed, full-height doors.

37

The palette of materials is controlled: blue limestone and European oak; matt white lacquer joinery and paintwork; soft gray Venetian plaster for the curved plate wall, and steel and glass for the rest.

Initially nervous that the white finishes would result in an environment that was too clinical, the clients are now effusive about the tranquility and calm of their luminous, light-filled home, high above the traffic of London.

CAIRNHILL PLAZA APARTMENT

SCDA Architects

This 2300-square-foot apartment is located on the fifth floor of a residential building.

The renovation included the conversion of an existing bedroom into a family/media room area by a large sandblasted glass sliding door that had to be transported into the apartment by crane, as it was too large for the elevator. A water feature and reflecting pool were incorporated into the terrace, adding a peaceful aspect to the treetop views beyond. The kitchen renovation includes extensive use of stainless steel and black granite for the cabinets, counter tops, and appliances.

Other materials used in the renovation include beige limestone internal flooring, white volax marble in the bathrooms, teak wood as a feature in the bedroom, and rustic white granite for external flooring.

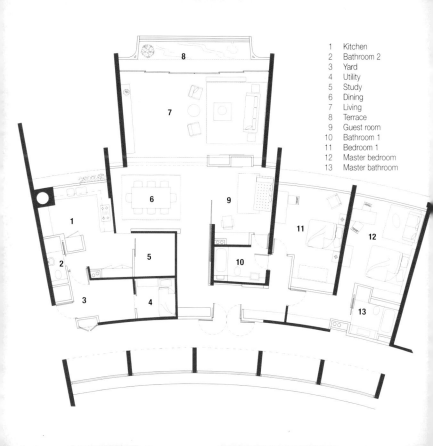

1   Kitchen
2   Bathroom 2
3   Yard
4   Utility
5   Study
6   Dining
7   Living
8   Terrace
9   Guest room
10 Bathroom 1
11 Bedroom 1
12 Master bedroom
13 Master bathroom

CITY LOFT

Paramita Abirama Istasadhya

Located in the main business area of Jakarta, Indonesia, and designed as a place for work or play, this two-story loft apartment offers a sense of serenity high above the city. A high curtain wall on one side of the loft enhances the sense of spaciousness while an enormous glass window allows both levels of the apartment to look out to the magnificent cityscape. The window wall also allows maximum penetration of natural daylight throughout most of the space, and in enclosed spaces such as the bathroom, a glass insert on the upper part of the wall provides more natural light.

The first floor of the apartment accommodates the living area, dining room, and a compact kitchen. The second floor, or the mezzanine, is a private area reserved for a bedroom, a luxurious dressing room, and a bathroom.

If the loft is used as a working space, then this second-floor section can be transformed into a professional or executive suite, while the first floor can be adapted to accommodate staff and working stations.

Architectural elements such as a timber and a glass partition as well as clever furniture groupings define the function of each area without using unnecessary solid walls. Carefully chosen artworks and home accessories also help to separate areas.

CLARENDON TOWERS PENTHOUSE

Rori Homes

Situated on level 27 of an apartment tower in Melbourne's inner-city Southbank precinct, this penthouse offers spectacular views over the city, Port Phillip Bay, and Albert Park Lake, where the Formula One Grand Prix is held. The challenge was to create an interior that would be as impressive as the vista it looked out over, although the owner brought to the table many of his own design ideas, having been inspired by the grandeur of penthouses in places like Dubai.

The open-plan interior was created from the merger of two neighboring apartments and the amalgamation resulted in a lavish floor plan that features five bathrooms, three spacious bedrooms, including a principal suite with a built-in library and his-and-hers bathroom, an entrance hall, a gymnasium, and an entertainment area with a commercial-size bar. There is also a separate office with its own boardroom, plus four outdoor balconies for alfresco entertaining.

Two laser-cut, rust-coated wall features were imported from China for the formal lounge, while wandoo timber recycled from a 100-year-old wool storage shed in Western Australia was used for the floor of the bar area. These 'rustic' surfaces were the perfect backdrop for the cutting-edge technology that was incorporated into much of the interior, blending old and new together in a curiously symbiotic fit. As befitting a modern penthouse, the techno-gadgets include portable touch pads enabling remote control from any room, an elaborate fiber-optics lighting system that changes the color of the bar depending on the mood required, and a drop-down LCD screen, along with nine televisions and 20 built-in speakers.

Topped off with a baby grand piano, set theatrically against a stunning city skyline backdrop, the apartment is a perfect play area high above the hustle and bustle of the city.

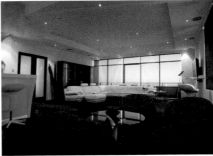

COLOR AND LIGHT

Brunete Fraccaroli

Color, light, and function are the main characteristics of the work of Brunete Fraccaroli, a leading Brazilian interior designer. This apartment could be in any part of the world but it is located in São Paulo, where the variety of different people and tastes is very influential. The play of light and color and the mixture of materials together create a contemporary language.

The entrance hall, where white Carrara marble meets the light wood floor, is a feature of the architect's repertoire. The owner, a very famous television personality in Brazil, wanted a place where he and his family could rest after a busy day of work. At the same time he also wanted a place where contemporary aspects would be the most important: light rooms that are full of color. The peaceful white color contrasting with the strong orange and red colors of the laminated mirror in the fireplace room is one of the most perfect contrasts in the apartment.

The main design is based on the functional aspects of the spaces and on the contrast between the different colors and materials.

DARLING POINT APARTMENT

Stanic Harding Architects

This doughnut-shaped, 155-square-meter apartment was stripped back and redesigned to celebrate the potential of an unhindered circular journey. The space was designed to ooze out to the perimeter while keeping the core unencumbered. A series of sliding doors pull away from the core into the radiating walls that define individual rooms. Being conscious of the spaces between the ends of these walls and the core, the edges were curved and splayed to counter the regular walnut core paneling. Connecting all these spaces allowed for wonderful vistas to the city skyline, the harbour, or the tree canopies.

The existing entry from the lift lobby led straight into a services cabinet. This was reconfigured to provide a direct connection to the bay and the external balcony. A bedroom was removed to allow the combined living/dining spaces to enjoy an unencumbered view. The existing services cabinet was clad in a curvaceous metallic silver paneling to create display niches, storage, a fold-down bar and housing for sound equipment. This once unsightly element is now a very useful space-maker, separating the television zone from the general area.

The paneled core is designed to contrast with the glazed perimeter and to ground the occupant. The core accommodates laundries, robes, and storage that are hidden to the casual visitor. Mirror paneling bends the space, giving glimpses of the view. The scheme celebrates the circle and the edge conditions that result from planning within it.

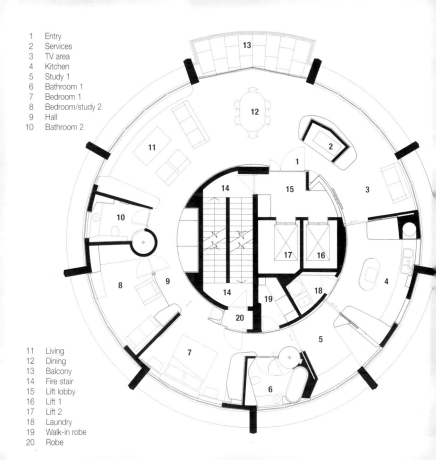

1   Entry
2   Services
3   TV area
4   Kitchen
5   Study 1
6   Bathroom 1
7   Bedroom 1
8   Bedroom/study 2
9   Hall
10   Bathroom 2
11   Living
12   Dining
13   Balcony
14   Fire stair
15   Lift lobby
16   Lift 1
17   Lift 2
18   Laundry
19   Walk-in robe
20   Robe

EGREJA APARTMENT

Rosenbaum—Arquitetura e Interiores

At 140 square meters, this is not a large apartment by São Paulo standards. Very cozy, and designed with contemporary Brazilian flair, it is the result of close collaboration between the architect and the client, a collector of Brazilian art, who is also passionately moved by Brazilian popular music. Previously a city base for the client who lived on a farm, the apartment was transformed when she decided to make the city her home. A priority was to incorporate her extensive Brazilian art collection, which has been arranged like a patchwork around the apartment.

The walls of the apartment were opened to make one large space for the living, dining, and kitchen areas. A touch of whimsy is the poetry on the walls, part of a very famous song from well-known Brazilian composer and singer, Chico Buarque de Hollanda. Snippets appear in the living space, in the entrance, and in the bedroom; poetry for a poetic soul.

The color palette is deliberately eclectic: the vibrant and colorful paintings of famous Brazilian artists contrast with the brown walls of the living space; the orange color of the curtain and an Egg chair enhances the black details in some items of furniture, which in turn anticipates the contemporary black kitchen.

Amou daquela vez
como se fosse a última
e cada filho seu como se
fosse o único
dançou e gargalhou
como se ouvisse música

ERIC STREET APARTMENT

Overman & Zuideveld Pty Ltd

The 250-square-meter layout of this apartment creates an open-plan living area that relates to the 39-square-meter, north-facing balcony adjoining it. Large areas of floor-to-ceiling glass between internal and external living areas make the internal areas feel larger while bi-folding doors and large sliding doors allow internal and external areas to meld together into one large space.

A wide gallery space replaces the conventional passage linking the living areas to other rooms within the apartment. This space feels like a room in itself with doors set back from the wall face in recesses, and the doors are located to provide maximum wall areas for artwork. A large pivot door allows the gallery to be separated from the entry if desired.

Through the use of raised ceiling areas and bulkheads, the large open-plan living area is zoned into living and dining/kitchen spaces. This manipulation of the ceiling also allows for variations in light source within each space. The kitchen has a 'built-in' feel, rather than the look of cabinetwork added to the envelope.

The cabinetwork is a dominant feature of the living space and provides a restrained non-utilitarian backdrop. There was a deliberate decision to avoid the use of wall tiles within the kitchen. Cabinetwork in the living room and entry was designed as an extension of the palette within the kitchen.

The materials selected for the interior of the apartment are generally from the gray color palette. Micro Cielo resin-based terrazzo was selected for the bench tops because of its durability and color. Queensland walnut was chosen as the timber veneer to add some warmth to the gray and neutral tones selected elsewhere. The dark carpet provides a strong visual base for the selected furniture. The ceilings of the balcony areas are lined with 'stressed' oak, which provides a weathered, driftwood feel, reflecting the beachside location.

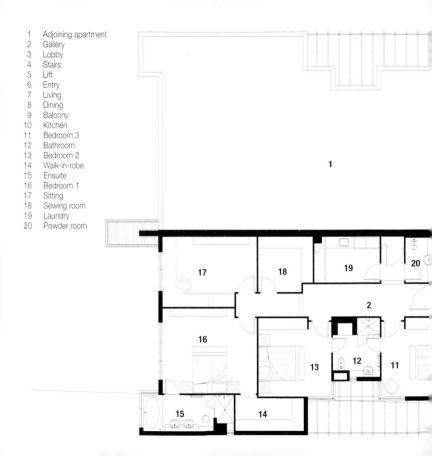

1   Adjoining apartment
2   Gallery
3   Lobby
4   Stairs
5   Lift
6   Entry
7   Living
8   Dining
9   Balcony
10   Kitchen
11   Bedroom 3
12   Bathroom
13   Bedroom 2
14   Walk-in-robe
15   Ensuite
16   Bedroom 1
17   Sitting
18   Sewing room
19   Laundry
20   Powder room

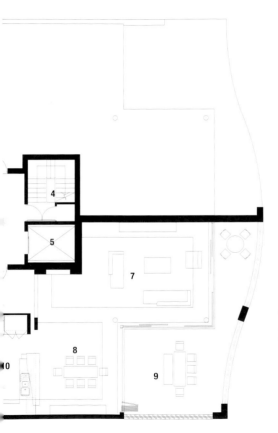

FASHIONABLE LIVING

Gilberto Cioni & Olegário de Sá—Arquitetura e Interiores

The owner of this apartment spends part of the year in São Paulo, and part in Italy. His busy schedule required a very relaxed place to be when in São Paulo. The architects proposed a contemporary place with solid lines; sober, but very 2000s.

The 280-square-meter apartment has two floors with the living, dining and kitchen on the first floor, and the bedroom and television room on the second. A terrace covers almost the entire second floor, with 120 square meters of open space and a panoramic view of the city.

The walls on the first floor are white, with chamois in the dining space. A comfortable red couch breaks the monochromatic palette. The modern furniture for the first floor is a perfect match with the natural-fiber objects on the second.

The living area encourages conversation between friends with the red couch and an Egg chair. Behind the red couch a lounge space was formed with three ecological wood and leather chairs and a black lacquered coffee table. The black dining table forms a niche with its six wood and black leather chairs.

The special white gypsum roof covers all of the first floor and interacts with the original slab, forming geometric forms for the lighting. A white cement stair painted in white epoxy links both floors, and becomes another decorative feature, as does the black ebony door just below the staircase.

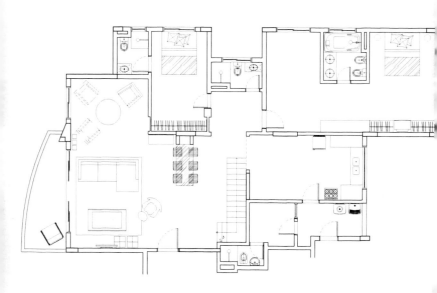

SEATTLE, WASHINGTON, USA

GLASS APARTMENT

Olson Sundberg Kundig Allen Architects

Glass, art, light, and water are recurring themes in this home for a collector of Northwest and Asian art. Using Puget Sound and the Pacific Ocean as a metaphorical setting to unite the collector's interests, the house takes on an organic and aqueous feeling. Located in a typical residential tower with relatively low ceiling heights, one of the design challenges was to create a sense of height and an open quality within a very tight envelope. Curved elements—made using floor-to-ceiling, cast-glass walls, some of which incorporate glass display shelving for art—were introduced to reference shapes found in nature, and to draw the eye away from the physical limits of the space and onto the contents. Interior separations were kept to a minimum, or rendered in glass, to visually unify the interior.

Entering the foyer is like stepping out of a diving bell into an undersea world with bronze gates marking the threshold. Inside, light passing through the glass walls, as well as coming from within them, gives the interior spaces a luminous Northwest glow. Ceiling areas are lit to appear as if seen from below the surface of the water, further reinforcing the aquatic feeling of the space. Cabinetry and construction details are highly crafted, reflecting the owner's dedication to the arts and crafts tradition of the Northwest. Much of the furniture was custom-designed by Jim Olson and finds its inspiration in objects found while beachcombing: driftwood, lily pads (sawmill castoffs), and sea-polished glass. The architecture is intended to work in concert with the art—to hold the art but not be completely subordinated by it.

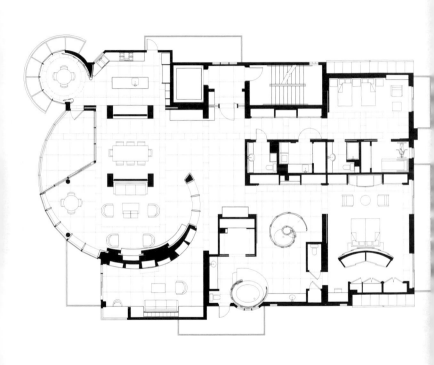

THE GRAND PENTHOUSE

Paramita Abirama Istasadhya

This three-story penthouse is located on the top floors of the Four Seasons Residences in Jakarta, Indonesia. It was designed around the themes of richness and glamor, which are reflected in the use of materials such as American walnut paneling and Italian marble flooring.

Set over three floors, each connected by a grand staircase as well as a customized walnut panel interior lift that floats between the floors, the penthouse comprises a first floor open-plan living area. Here, a spectacular panoramic view of Jakarta welcomes the guests as they enter the living room, and an intimate cigar room that provides a more private space.

Most of the second floor is occupied by the master bedroom, which maintains its privacy by having a separate lounge and foyer, both of which connect to the music room. The color palette—one of soft beiges and deep maroons—was chosen for its rich sophistication, while crystal fixtures for the lighting add further glitz to an already glamorous setting. There is also a second bedroom on this second floor, while a further bedroom is located on the top floor.

GYMNASIUM RESIDENCE

Gwathmey Siegel & Associates Architects

This 6000-square-foot apartment is located in the former gymnasium of the original Beaux Arts New York City Police Headquarters building.

The intention was to physically maintain and visually exploit the volumetric integrity and structural expression of the existing barrel-vaulted space, while adding a master bedroom suite and study/library balcony, and integrating an eclectic painting and sculpture collection.

On the main level of the 25-foot-high, steel-trussed volume, is the multi-use living/dining/entertainment/gallery articulated by custom-designed, space-defining furniture. At the east end of the space is the master bedroom suite and study/library balcony accessed by an exposed stair, which rotates at the landing and runs parallel, behind the existing longitudinal steel truss, to attic guest bedrooms over the kitchen, master baths, and dressing rooms.

The study/library balcony is suspended under the east end of the barrel vault and revealed from the master bedroom below by a continuous radial skylight in the floor, expressing its separation while maintaining the volumetric extension.

The floor of the balcony defines the bedroom ceiling, floating asymmetrically within the existing orthogonal building frame, articulating its objectiveness and sectional variation.

Three large skylights were inserted into the south side of the barrel-vaulted roof, providing natural light into the longitudinal internal façade of the space and revealing the classic building pediment above.

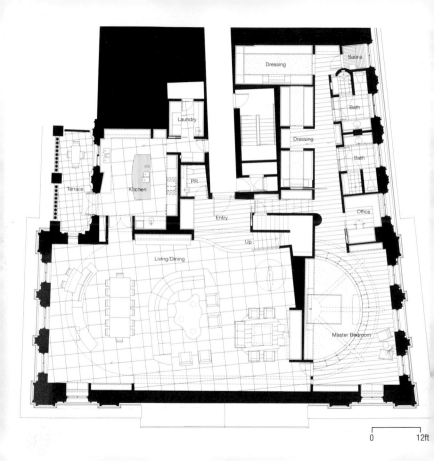

Dressing

Sauna

Laundry

Bath

Dressing

Terrace

Kitchen

PR

Bath

Entry

Office

Up

Living/Dining

Master Bedroom

0   12ft

Major materials used include Bateig limestone and oak plank floors, Venetian plaster walls, perforated glass fiber-reinforced gypsum, panels and plaster ceilings with white lacquer cabinets. The color palette comprises warm white walls, honey-stained wide plank oak floors, beige-gray limestone, brushed stainless steel, white lacquer cabinets, bluestone countertops, and walnut-stained cherry cabinets in the library.

HIGH STYLE IN SÃO PAULO

Studio Helena Viscomi

The owners of this 980-square-meter duplex apartment requested architect Helena Viscomi's help in remodeling their home by giving it 'a little flair and imagination.' Helena was struck by the living room's limitless possibilities. The huge space gave her the opportunity to relocate and organize all the objects of Oriental, Brazilian, and European art that the couple has collected from their worldwide travels.

The clients have a very active social life so it was important to create a well-organized space. Warm in spirit, but slightly formal was the design brief. The two-story penthouse was designed some years ago, with two distinct levels: the first floor houses a covered terrace around the living room, the informal and formal dining rooms, five bedrooms, the kitchen, and the service area and dog's area. Upstairs is the master bedroom with a private bathroom and private terrace, the home theater space, a bar, a swimming pool, a barbecue, and the solarium from which one can admire a view of São Paulo city on the horizon.

The formal living room on the first floor is very classic and traditional, where the fine artworks are a perfect match for the silk sofas and curtains. The sweeping veranda can be used as an additional living room with chairs and sofas, or as a dining room, with its table for relaxed meals.

The home theater on the second floor, with its black and red color scheme contrasts to the traditional living room downstairs. Although it seems to be part of a completely different apartment, it fits perfectly with the needs of the different generations that live together.

HIGHLAND CONDOMINIUM

Olson Sundberg Kundig Allen Architects

Occupying the sixth floor of a mid-rise condominium on the south slope of Seattle's Queen Anne Hill, the Blem residence overlooks the downtown skyline and waterfront. The Space Needle commands the foreground, and Mount Rainier dominates the distance.

The owners, a couple with grown children, wanted refuge from the stress of their vocations. The husband manufactures medical imaging equipment, and this interior was designed to embody their love of clean lines and precision. It is restrained, thanks to a monochromatic color palette and polished, elegant materials. Its plan is also simple and exact: a main room for living, cooking, eating, and entertaining, extends into subsidiary spaces such as bedrooms, a bathroom, dressing, and exercise areas. The absence of conventional walls and doors makes the moderately sized space seem larger.

A curving, visually porous entry wall of perforated steel leads the eye into the apartment and creates a moiré pattern that changes as the viewer moves. Private space is separated from public by freestanding storage modules, sheathed in perforated metal, surmounted by uplights, and supported by steel brackets that extend from floor to ceiling. This row of volumes forms an axis that extends from the entry to the window wall at the opposite end of the apartment.

Primary materials include polished granite, glass block, and stainless steel; the latter forming the fireplace surround, much of the kitchen and bathroom, the bedroom headboard, and most of the flooring.

Details are highly crafted and articulated, and assume great prominence. The kitchen island, for example, is a sculptural plane of stainless steel tapering to a thin wafer at the end where it hangs from a suspended metal bar. In a city where interiors tend to be relaxed and organic, this apartment stands out with its finely honed Manhattan-like elegance.

HILL LOFT

Resolution: 4 Architecture

Located within a former industrial building in New York City's TriBeCa district, the Hill Loft is an exercise in efficiency of space and a response to existing conditions. Due to the limited square footage of the space, a design based around the simplicity of gesture was the only response.

Various programs are accommodated in large cabinetry units adhering to one edge of the loft, which span between massive steel-plate columns. Programmatic zones are inserted within these columns to occupy this irregular space. These include kitchen cabinetry, wine storage, a sleeping space, and an entertainment area.

The sculptural bar element created out of the kitchen island and dining table combo hovers in front of the thick, rhythmic wall of cabinetry. It is composed of a rectangular base on the kitchen side, which supports a site-cast, L-shaped concrete countertop, with a maple dining surface cantilevering forward from the solid portion toward the window at the south end of the loft.

Given the linear sequence of the space, the ceiling landscape acts to connect the living areas together. Beginning at the entry, flexible track-lighting weaves through the space, unwinding to an expansive view of lower Manhattan.

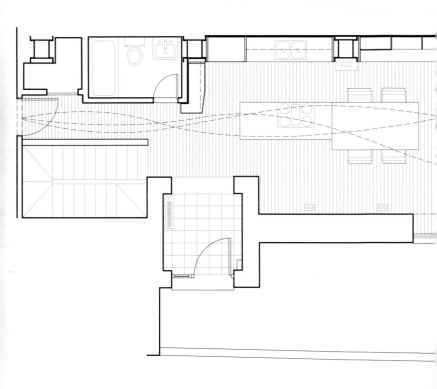

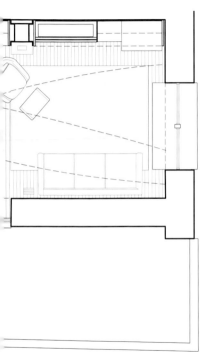

JACKSON APARTMENT

Stanic Harding Architects

Prior to renovation this 150-square-meter apartment presented a low central corridor and a land-locked entry. Rooms ran along the perimeter of the building thereby denying the occupant connection to views, light, and edge.

The apartment was opened by fusing circulation with habitable space. The planning allowed all major spaces to connect to the edge of the building and to views over Sydney Harbour. The incorporation of the external balcony and corridor space allowed for planning options that were not previously possible. The balcony now operates as a dining space but with the benefits of an outdoor space. It also links the main bedroom to the apartment in a way that reinforces its exclusion from the general living areas.

The design seeks to balance the connection to the extensive views and the focus on internal spaces. Joinery is used as a second layer to create elements that sometimes frame views and are sometimes the focus. These space-making elements are carefully detailed and connected; some are highly reflective and rich while others are plain and white. Color is used on walls and joinery furthest from the edge, with edge elements being white. Joinery wall paneling conceals services, storage, laundry, and bathroom areas from the casual visitor. Discovering some of these items/areas enhances the space's experiential qualities. The use of mirrors also extends space and brings in Sydney Harbour. The kitchen plays a central role as both space maker and viewing platform, reinforced by a change in floor level.

entry

bedroom 2

bathrm 2

hallway

study

ldy

dressing

bathrm 1

bedroom 1

kitchen

SW
balcony

living /
dining

SE
balcony

LOFT 6

Dale Jones-Evans Pty Ltd Architecture

Loft 6 is one of ten lofts forming part of the 50–54 Ann Street Warehouse Loft Conversion, which was also designed by the architect. The shell space was completely redesigned by the architect, and the new plan creates a seductive gallery for functional living while paying great attention to drama and light.

The approach was to restructure the ground area as a cavernous yet welcoming space and make the floor solid, so one felt grounded—earthed. The three-story void and main place of ascension was then reinforced through cantilevering and floating the main stairs, using slatted timbers for landings and bridges.

The interior utilizes a painterly palette of surfaces to offset the owners' art collection. The layout of bedrooms below and living spaces above generated the off-white to black-brown color scheme. The spaces below are cave-like and white, while the higher-level floors are timber and stained off-black, contrasting with the solid white cavern below. The dark ceilings and floors in the living spaces also temper the intensity of the east–west light, visually extending the space toward the external deck and water garden. This water garden is replenished through a talon of copper as part of a cooling and decorative device for the living spaces.

In the sunroom above, light is filtered through a bamboo screen to reinforce the presence of light and sky. The roof level acts as a place to connect with non-urban elements in full view of the city and is also an ideal place for contemplation.

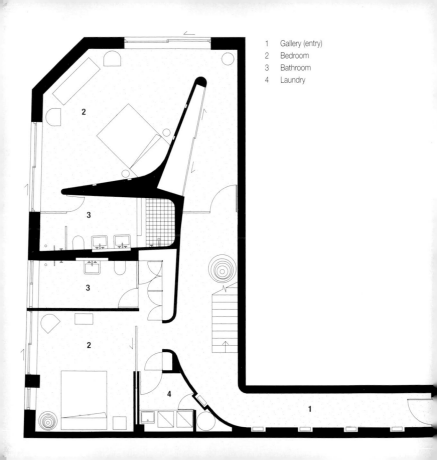

1 Gallery (entry)
2 Bedroom
3 Bathroom
4 Laundry

Photography: Paul Gosney

SYDNEY, NEW SOUTH WALES, AUSTRALIA

MCMILLAN APARTMENT

Stanic Harding Architects

This project involved the creation of a two-story penthouse apartment in Jacksons Landing, Pyrmont, in Sydney. As part of the Jackson's Landing development, the building was converted and expanded into a contemporary apartment building.

The penthouse's owner wanted to develop the apartment beyond the basic layout that had originally been proposed. This involved the full redesign of the apartment, as well as any necessary alterations to the main building structure.

The main public living areas are located on the lower level, along with the master bedroom and guest bedroom, while the top level accommodates a family room, a study, a laundry, and an expansive roof terrace offering panoramic views to the city and the harbor.

The apartment is accessed via a lift that leads directly into an entry space allowing a controlled separation from the living spaces on the lower level and the views beyond. The living dining and kitchen areas are all connected as one space, which, in turn, connects to the main north-facing terrace.

A wood-burning fireplace is located within the main lounge/dining area, which also encompasses the open stair assembly that links to the upper level. To extend the connection of the living area to the external terrace the window wall was modified to allow a clear opening of 8 meters, allowing the apartment to be fully opened up and extended outside.

A third bedroom was connected to the main living area by the introduction of a large sliding door that parks within the fireplace block. This space becomes a more intimate extension of the living area offering an informal study/ reading area.

The kitchen is closely connected to the main public space, avoiding any isolation of the cook, however a glazed sliding screen was introduced to offer privacy as required.

A pivot door connecting to the main window wall offers access to the master bedroom and ensuite area. This area can also be accessed directly from the main entry area of the apartment. Privacy can be obtained as required by the use of a further sliding door which parks out of view when not in use.

The open stair visually connects the two levels by means of a combination of voids. The upper level houses a family room and a study area, which is a more private family retreat zone. The accommodation on this level also connects to an external terrace, which is to be developed as an intimate roof garden to accommodate an external kitchen with barbecue facilities.

TERRACE
CONC TILES

TERRACE
CONC TILES

TERRACE
CONC TILES

BED 1

KITCHEN

DINING

LIVING

FIREPLACE

HALL

LOBBY

STORE

BED 2

WC

HWD

GARBAGE

ENSUITE

LIFT 3

LIFT 4

HALL

FHR

CONC

EDB

BED 3

STAIR 3

STAIR 4

MILSONS POINT APARTMENT

Stanic Harding Architects

The owners of this apartment in a former multi-story office building in Sydney's Milsons Point work locally but retreat to a holiday house interstate on weekends, and thus required this space to serve as their week-day home.

The apartment's original plan denied them a connection to the view and light by stacking bedrooms along most of the perimeter. The kitchen was also effectively disconnected from its dining area and the narrow living space by being tucked into the rear of the interior.

The plan was to reconfigure the space by stripping away everything and taking the apartment back to its bare shell. The new design then allowed for a considered entry sequence, while providing clear separation of public and private spaces.

One of the three bedrooms was relocated at the back of the apartment to where the kitchen had once stood. This allowed for the two remaining bedrooms to be increased in size and connect more successfully to light and views. The public spaces then increased in size along the perimeter window wall, while the third bedroom became a guest/study space raised above the main floor level and defined by a different floor finish.

ensuite

bed 3
/study

entry

dressing

bathroom

kitchen
/dining

hall

bed 1

bed 2

living

balcony

he kitchen/dining space was brought into the main ving/entry zone to clearly define public areas from rivate. The main wall was clad in full-height mirror panels hat immediately doubled the perception of available pace and reflected the harbor view. The kitchen now ffords views that would have been previously impossible. chocolate timber floor, laid in an opposing grid, defines ne main spaces, while very plush shag pile carpet defines ne lounging area and the bedroom spaces.

Joinery plays an important role in the transformations, sometimes highlighting edges and other times defining spaces. The main kitchen joinery, for example, is a rectangular pod that divides kitchen and guestroom/study. It houses the main kitchen bench and associated storage on one side, general storage at each end, and the study on the other side. A built-in dining table reflects the apartment's use, as it was not conceived as a place for extensive entertaining; more as a home for the working week.

MODERN STYLE

Gui Mattos Arquitetura

Architect Gui Mattos' client was accustomed to living in and planning big, open houses so it was a challenge to plan the smaller space of an apartment. Fortunately, the close affinity between architect and client made the transition a positive experience.

The owner, an enthusiastic collector of modern art and design, wanted something to fit his contemporary lifestyle. The first thing to do was to make the apartment as cozy and home-like as his previous residence.

The architect opened the walls to make one large space for the living and dining areas. Fabulous objects d'art and artworks make this a balanced, unified space. A feature of the apartment was the abundance of natural light, which contributes to the overall ambience, especially in the living areas, with their floor-to-ceiling windows.

Some significant changes to the original plan were made to adapt the space to the owner's style of living. Some interior finishes were changed, to enhance the display of the paintings and other works of art.

NYCHAY LOFT

Resolution: 4 Architecture

Located in a new loft building in the historic neighborhood of Soho, in downtown New York City, this project was designed for a single young professional in search of an urban enclave. The design attempts to address the classic loft problem of open-plan living versus partitioned intimacy through the use of contrast, and the employment of a sophisticated, high-end, residential-style interior within the primitiveness of an original industrial building.

On one edge, a dense complex box contains the kitchen, mechanical, and secondary spaces, all of which are separated from the public areas. The bathrooms, bedroom, and dressing area are packed-out to allow the continuity of the 66-foot-long space and its 50 linear feet of windows overlooking Soho's roofscapes. A system of sliding and translucent partitions allows the bedroom to be closed off.

On the other edge, both the built-in and free-standing furniture pieces occupy the continuous space, modulating the raw volume into a coherent place for living. The office area is identified by the mahogany desk, the dining room by the rosewood table, the kitchen by the teak island, and the living room by a wenge wall.

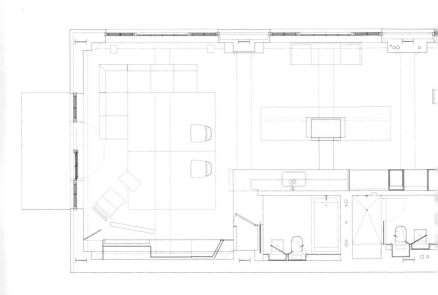

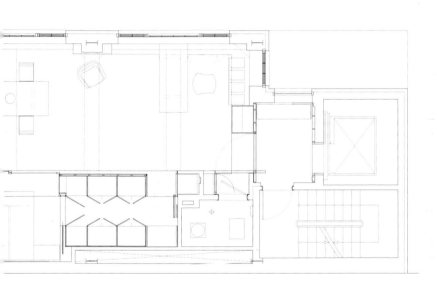

OLIVER LANE PENTHOUSE

DesignInc Melbourne

The brief for this project called for a reinvention of the interior of an existing penthouse in the Melbourne CBD. Previously renovated in the mid 1990s, the existing interior had become tired and dated. The client requested a timeless design that would not date so readily. The project included upgrading the existing kitchen and designing a new bathroom. Through structural alteration and furniture specification, the project succeeded in meeting the client's requirements and creating a light, bright, inviting environment. Combining new furniture items with reupholstered existing pieces, the design demonstrates a successful synergy between new and old.

Classic modern furniture pieces were made the focus and the upholstery palette was one that concentrated more on texture and depth than color, giving the apartment an added dimension in tactility. New lighting systems were also specified to further enhance the open plan, while the replacement of internal walls with frameless glass panels maximized natural light and promoted visual connections between rooms and city skylines.

A highlight of the apartment is the ensuite bathroom that features frameless glass panels, stainless steel mosaic tiles and a ceramic 'box' vanity. The minimal palette used in the refurbishment artistically blends all elements of the apartment, old and new, into a contemporary reinvention of the penthouse.

PERRATON APARTMENT

Stephen Varady Architecture

The design for this city apartment set out to explore an intensive, practical use of space through sculptural and formal exploration, and to not only make a 40-square-meter apartment more practical and functional, but also make it appear larger.

The design approach treats the interior as a series of intersecting, white rectangular prisms—initially suggested by the strong rectilinear form of the existing envelope. The intent was to hide what was not necessary, only bringing it to life when needed. For example, the kitchen does not look like a kitchen but a sculptural wall of intersecting elements, stepping back and forth to accommodate storage, appliances, and plumbing, with certain parts folding down, sliding out, or opening to reveal the various functions related to the preparation of food.

The design also explores other ideas for saving space. Select sections of the non-load-bearing walls, as well as the bedroom and bathroom doors have been removed and replaced with large sliding panels. The cantilevered dining table folds away to become part of the overall composition, allowing clear floor space when it is not in use. The television has been encased in a sculptural cabinet and suspended from a box on the ceiling, which completely conceals the power and antenna cables. A sliding track allows it to glide along the ceiling.

A number of strategically placed mirrors also allow the apartment to appear more than what it is. The major mirror beside the main northern window not only extends the perception of space, but brings a previously limited view of Sydney Harbour right inside the apartment.

The kinetic potential of spaces intersecting is consciously explored; thus, the design is never fixed, never static, allowing the apartment to vary in size, proportion and mood depending on the required or desired function.

POTTER'S PAD

Resolution: 4 Architecture

Located in New York's Chelsea neighborhood, this 1400-square-foot loft renovation responds to the client's reductive lifestyle. The main volume is sheathed by a series of planes intended to articulate the edges and thresholds of the space. Within this volume, zones of use are suggested by the placement of specific planes of material. A raised plane of concrete ceiling panels identifies the living zone. Flanked by an anchored wall of steel and a floating wall of plaster, the dining zone is registered by a penetrating wedge of light from above, while a slipped plane of stone defines the fireplace to one side. Kitchen cabinets and appliances occupy a bite out of the central core and form another edge to the main open volume. Kitchen and dining zones are unified by a series of dancing rectangular bars of light that are carved into the ceiling above.

Thresholds of the space are layered with planes that slide, pivot, and roll. The sliding 'front door' provides security via a custom steel panel notched for hardware and light switches. The pivoting bedroom door provides privacy from within, while allowing light and a continuous brick wall to slip past, connecting the full length of the loft. Rolling perforated window scrims diffuse sunlight and provide privacy from the outside, while maintaining a view of the street.

Additional 'planes of use' fold, cantilever, and divide. An additional sleeping plane for guests folds into a concealed cabinet in the living zone. The master bed is composed of several cantilevered planes, and storage cabinets are accented with aluminum dividers. Sliced with aluminum, a slab of Baltic ply is used as a dining table that is equipped with industrial casters. It has the ability to roll up against the kitchen island and clear the space for impromptu dancing.

197

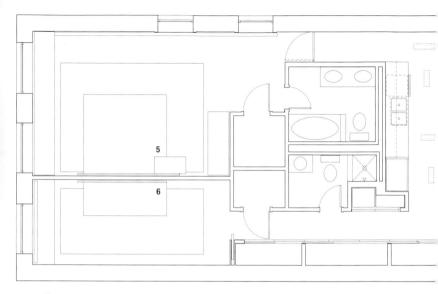

1 Entry
2 Living
3 Dining
4 Kitchen
5 Bedroom
6 Guest bedroom

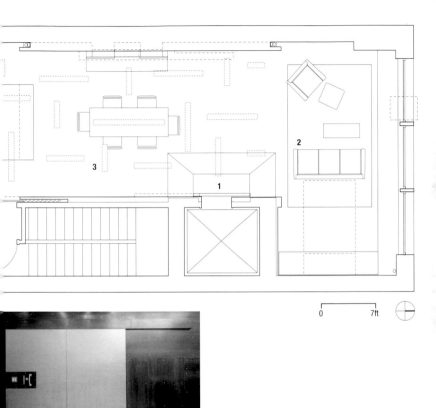

1

2

3

0   7ft

Q LOFT (LOFT FOR A SUPERHERO)

Resolution: 4 Architecture

The Q-Loft project was the complete renovation of a loft for Joe Quesada, the editor-in-chief of Marvel Comics in New York, and his family. It is located in a former industrial building in New York's Chelsea neighborhood and occupies an entire floor with full window exposure and dynamic urban views on three sides. Due to the depth of the extremely large floor plate, the private living zones are "packed out" on three exterior walls. The public zones then interweave between these zones, stitching them together.

The master bedroom is situated on a view axis with the Empire State Building, with a glassed-in master closet and bathroom situated behind. The guest bedroom, child's room, and play room are located on the opposite side of the loft. All of these private spaces are provided with overhead interior windows to bring natural light to the interior of the floor plate. In between these private zones are the semi-private home theater, the entry, the powder room, and an artist's studio. The large object void of the theater may be dissolved into the public space by opening the large glass sliding doors.

The open public areas include the kitchen, dining room, and living area. The semi-private studio/powder room bar resolves in the kitchen and opens into the larger living space, combining programs of cooking and entertaining within the apartment. Dividing as well as connecting the kitchen and living areas is a freestanding island. The living area remains open, allowing both the views of the city and maximum natural light to enter the loft space.

To accommodate Mr. Quesada's large collection of comic artifacts, a number of built-ins are also included in the studio and on the back of the theater for display. The shelves on the theater are acrylic and are internally lighted.

RON'S LOFT

Resolution: 4 Architecture

To begin with, the owner of this New York loft wanted to only replace his kitchen cabinets and maintain existing partitions. Later, he decided to reorganize his entire interior by opening up the loft and creating a more dynamic living space.

The long and narrow container-style space, typical of loft spaces in New York, was reconfigured into separate living zones comprising an office, a living room, a dining room, a kitchen, and a bedroom. One long edge of the loft was redesigned with cabinetry to offer continuous storage for the bedroom and kitchen, as well as a sideboard for dining. The other edge encompassed bathrooms and additional cabinetry.

This 'packing out' of the perimeter created a swath of space that now contains a new hearth, which both separates and unites the public and private spaces. Designed as a stationary yet operable element, this hearth contains sliding Polygal and Unistrut panels that refract natural light deep into the loft. On the bedroom side, it becomes the headboard for a built-in bed, creating privacy in the bedroom. On the kitchen side, the range and its exhaust hood become a central element within the space, creating a focus for informal entertainment.

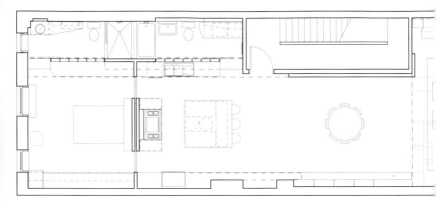

Each public space is further defined by the occupation of a custom piece of furniture, which accommodates seating arrangements of varying heights. The kitchen island is a movable square butcher's block composed of Metrowire and maple flooring while the dining table is a circle of three layers of chamfered Baltic birch plywood with aluminum inlays.

Each of the planes separating the rooms are made of translucent materials, allowing further penetration of light and creating an ephemeral relationship between private, semi-private, and public spaces.

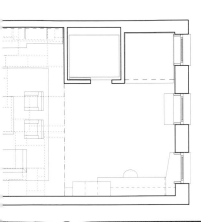

RUSHCUTTERS BAY APARTMENT

Chenchow Little Architects

This apartment is on the top floor of a new multi-unit residential building on the water at Rushcutters Bay. The building did not respond to its location or the user, but provided a generic minimum standard dwelling with a tiny floor space. The client required the entire interior to be refitted (except the bathrooms), but the challenge was to provide a contemporary interior that gave the illusion of more space, and provided flexibility and storage.

Three main elements are used in this scheme: the white walls and cabinetry, which wrap around the periphery of the apartment; two dark timber volumes within the space, which contain the laundry and the kitchen; and the mirrored wall.

The three elements have very different qualities and have been strategically located to enhance the sense of space. The white walls wrap around the dark volumes, constantly leading the eye into the distance. The mirror, used at the point of greatest spatial restriction, enhances the sensation of space through reflection. Long continuous lines run through the apartment in the floor, ceiling, and walls to enhance the sense of space. The lines continue through different functional zones. Continuous lines of aluminum extruded channels and white limestone run across the gray stone floor. Some house plumbing, electrical services and sliding door tracks; others are ornamental. Continuous lines in the ceiling house down-lights and sliding door tracks.

The horizontal shelf running across the western wall moves through the kitchen, dining and lounge zones in the apartment. The vertical lines on the western wall in the form of blade light columns, and the eastern wall in the form of recessed light shafts, provide continuity and structure to the main space, bridging the different ceiling heights and also enhancing the vertical. The blade light columns occur in the kitchen, dining and living spaces. The detailing system is continuous through each zone.

SISKIND SPACE

Resolution: 4 Architecture

Located on New York's famous Broadway between Union Square and the Flatiron District, this loft renovation exploits the potential of its unique corner condition through reductive means. Space is created through the use of two cabinetry volumes, which float within the large loft, permitting the two windowed perimeter walls to be fully experienced both visually and physically. The two volumes are disengaged from the perimeter walls and other adjacent construction through the use of enormous customized aluminum and glass doors, which either pivot or slide into dissolution.

One of the volumes accommodates the pragmatics of kitchen storage and equipment on one side, and book/media storage on the other, acting as a buffer between the kitchen/living space and the more private media/guest room. It strongly defines the public spaces by providing a background for the hub of activity that is the oversized kitchen island, around which the activities of cooking and entertaining converge. Simultaneously, the design sets up the sitting area at the corner of the space, while registering the dining area on the other.

The second element, a floating, reductive wood volume surrounded by the silence of frosted glass on three sides, serves as a buffer between the dining area and the master bedroom, while accommodating storage on the bedroom side. It acts as an elegant background to the dining table, expressing its formality.

The end result is a delicate balance between free-plan and formal stage setting, allowing the nature of both space and program to be fully expressed while achieving absolute synchrony between the two.

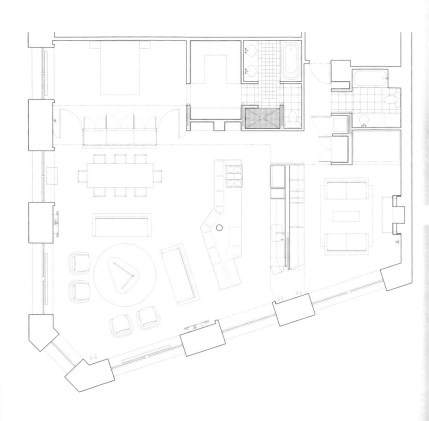

SOHO LOFT

aardvarchitecture

This 3000-square-foot loft renovation deals with the relationship between different scales of rooms—flexible, open spaces, and smaller private rooms. Both are set against a backdrop of 19th-century decorative detail and beyond, views to lower and mid-town Manhattan. The design juxtaposes the view framed by the windows to the interpenetrating spaces of the apartment's interior. As one moves through the spaces, shifting long and short views are offered. The framed images shift from frontal to oblique, and back.

The project was structured in phases to contain costs, with the architects contracting directly for all finishes to maintain high quality.

SORRENTO

Steve Leung Designers Ltd.

A streamlined, minimalist tranquility is achieved in this apartment through contemporary and cosmopolitan styling, optimal spatial extension, and a relaxing atmosphere. Simple, clean lines and a tone-on-tone color scheme on furniture and furnishings contribute to a sophisticated look for the 140-square-meter interior. Lights penetrate through the adjustable louver panels, inspiring the linear arrangement. Visual linkage between the study and living room through the glass glazed walls helps to create the impression of space while maintaining individuality. The use of large windows on the side of the dining room creates a mirage for the apartment.

The use of different materials, such as sycamore wood and fabric, for walls and floorings enhances the rich texture. Accompanied by deliberate mood lighting, the unique character is carried through to every corner of the apartment.

STEEL LOFT

Gwathmey Siegel & Associates Architects

The goal with this apartment was to perceive the 'idea' of a single 4400-square-foot rectilinear volume, which is hierarchically modulated and articulated through the layering, horizontally and vertically, of the forms and space. The space, 110 feet long by 40 feet wide, has 14 (7 pairs) of south-facing windows on the seventh floor of a loft building in Chelsea.

A line of existing columns, 18 feet from the south façade, articulates the main circulation gallery. A second circulation zone, visual and actual, parallel to and along the south window wall, accesses more private spaces—study, master bedroom suite, and master bath—through a sequence of thick wall niches that accommodate sliding steel and patterned glass doors for privacy.

The ceiling height to the underside of the slab is 9 foot, 10 inches. Existing beams form a second ceiling layer and are the primary referential horizontal graphic through the entire space. Three ceiling/wall heights below the beams establish datums for primary and secondary walls, which do not engage the ceiling but float below, exaggerating the illusion of a higher space. These varying ceiling heights afford opportunities to conceal ambient indirect lighting, as well as air-conditioning ducts and grilles, and preserve the overall spatial continuity. Major materials used include gray limestone, maple wood flooring, warm white walls, Anigre wood panels/cabinet, cold rolled steel, and stainless steel.

The loft is a three-dimensional reinterpretation of a Mondrian; it is an architecture that is at once articulate, graphic, sublime, and calm. It is a space conceived as an 'excavation,' a carving away that results in an essentialness that is inherently sculptural—light-filled, dense and sequential, where nothing is added or redundant.

SYDNEY HARBOR APARTMENT

Stanic Harding Architects

This apartment is located on level 16 of a circular, 18-story-high tower in Darling Point and takes up the whole floor. The location allows occupants extensive views of the harbor, the famous Sydney Harbour Bridge, and the Opera House, however the existing apartment layout didn't take advantage of the potential 360-degree views the circular plan offers.

The intention was to maximize the apartment's potential and also its sense of space by reconfiguring it to allow for a continuous path through all the spaces. All doors between rooms now slide away into joinery to provide for an unencumbered journey. As well, the apartment was stripped back to its concrete shell and the spaces redesigned to be more radial than orthogonal. The location and its spectacular views were enhanced through the use of picture windows wherever possible. The use of joinery as the major way of defining individual spaces in lieu of walls gives the impression of a well-appointed yacht. The edges of these joinery pieces encourage the spaces to flow into each other and also 'soften' the lines.

The ceiling treatment—which comprises thin, flush-fitting fluorescent strips radiating out to the perimeter—is designed to enhance the circular interior while providing for a stronger and cleaner ceiling plane. The central core has also been modified and is now a curved shell made up of beautifully finished panels upholstered in a padded wool fabric. These are either fixed or are concealed doors to storage or robe areas. Vertical strip lighting located at set centers divides panels and provides feature or mood lighting. The overall feel of the apartment is quite understated as the light entering the space changes constantly and provides its own level of interest.

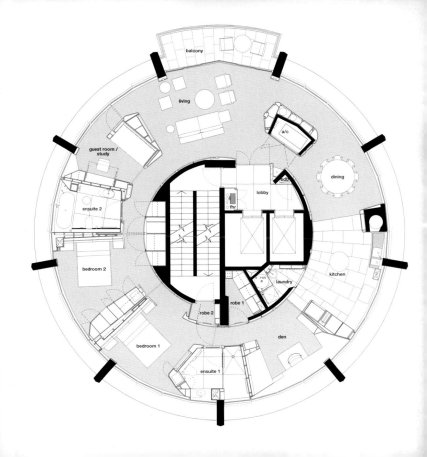

balcony

living

a/c

guest room / study

dining

lobby

ensuite 2

bed?

fhr

kitchen

bedroom 2

HW

laundry

robe 1

robe 2

den

bedroom 1

ensuite 1

THE LOFT OF FRANK AND AMY

Resolution: 4 Architecture

Designed for an art critic and a film editor, this 4800-square-foot loft is a bare, wide-open play space in New York City's gritty Hell's Kitchen neighborhood. Located in a former industrial building, the loft occupies an entire floor with full window exposure and dynamic urban views on three sides. The design enhances this industrial context by posing new construction as a single sculptural intervention within this existing space. This intervention becomes a compressed box of utility (containing the kitchen, mechanical and supportive spaces), that divides the public and private areas of the loft. A primary feature of the box is a series of huge sliding doors that can open the entire perimeter of the loft, or conversely, extend to the exterior walls to close off the bedrooms.

Photography: Paul Warchol

261

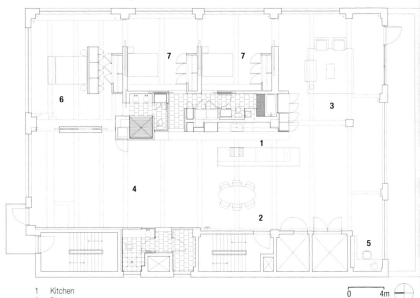

1 Kitchen
2 Dining
3 Living
4 Playing
5 Writing
6 Master bedroom
7 Bedroom

0   4m

THE UPPER EAST

Steve Leung Designers Ltd.

A strong contrasting theme of black and white throughout this 120-square-meter apartment signifies the distinctive character of cold winter, yet a little lime green neutralizes the chilly feel, creating an incredible harmony in a now welcoming environment.

Optimizing the living room's space and vision, a study is located adjacent, separated by a half-wall-height cabinet, which extends the living room while maintaining a private space for work and study. Opaque glass walls subtly crystallize the views and help highlight the surroundings, in the alternate adoption of white matte-painted walls.

Custom-made furniture with sharp outlines and stainless steel accents adds frosty feelings to match the furnishings. A tree-shaped artwork in the dining room not only coheres ideally with the winter ambience, but also adds extra sense of humor by its reversed echo in the master bedroom, extending the passionate black and white contrast to the utmost!

VILLA DEL ROSE

Reductive is the word that comes to mind to describe the clean, quiet tones in this refurbished two-level, 2000-square-foot apartment in an old maisonette block near the Botanical Gardens. The apartment is a longitudinal-shaped plan leading to a full-length balcony that opens out to a tree-filled view. SCDA's renovation of the apartment involved a number of structural changes—angles were straightened, a wall on the upper level was repositioned, and a storeroom on the lower level was omitted, but the main functional areas were left intact.

Plain-faced cabinetry of light timber elegantly demarcates the living and dining areas as well as providing storage and display. These fixtures imbue the spaces with a coherent, architectural character. The surfaces are kept uniformly 'clean'—even the light fittings, including those in the bathrooms, are all recessed, to de-emphasize the fixtures.

A 'wood-wall' in the dining room replaces an aluminum-framed frosted glass window that looks over the air-well. This plain-faced fixture is a unifying element in the overall reductive scheme. Daylight still enters but through two narrow vertical openings on the wood-wall, resulting in the dining room taking on a more sequestered character. In keeping with the architect's intention of 'clarifying the space,' existing structures are re-expressed, particularly the staircase and balcony. The staircase is reduced to just the timber treads, cantilevered into a specially thickened wall. The banister, a basic metal frame, has been retained for safety purposes. Water, a hallmark of SCDA's architecture, has been used in this project to enhance the design. The balcony becomes a reflection pool when filled with water, enhancing the owners' enjoyment of the greenery just outside.

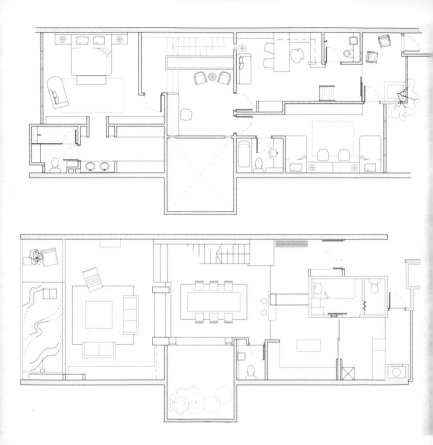

The awkward configuration of the existing shell space of this penthouse ultimately proved to be a positive generator for the design of this 2200-square-foot apartment.

A fluid series of distinct sub-spaces—defined by mood, function, volume, and outlook—have been created within an essentially open plan. A mezzanine floor inserted over the central wing of the plan provides the owner's gallery bedroom and bathroom as well as access, via a glazed slot, to an upper-level roof terrace.

A highly formalized double-height sitting area is counter balanced by the more enclosed dining and sitting spaces accommodated under the central mezzanine. The horizon view to the north from this latter space is accentuated by the linear geometry and the rising curved profile of the soffit. With north, east, and west outlooks, there is an ever-changing play of natural light within the space.

Within the formal sitting area, a double-height Mondrian-inspired grid of panels opens like an advent calendar to reveal media, emergency exit, storage and bar. The largest panel, in fact a wardrobe block accessed from its reverse face, slides electrically to enclose the gallery bedroom.

On the upper level, the master bedroom has specially designed storage for shirts and shoes and a television that rises up from a cupboard opposite the bed. Across the top-lit glazed hall, which also provides access to some 1200 square feet of external terraces, is the master bathroom, which incorporates a walk-in shower, over which are two large shower heads purpose-designed by the practice and featuring fiber optics to bathe the occupant in light as well as water.

Photography: Jeremy Lingard, Form Design Architecture & Matthew Weinreb

INDEX OF ARCHITECTS

INDEX OF ARCHITECTS